Reach for the Highest Star

A Real Psychic's True Life Experiences With God, Ghosts, Jesus, and a UFO Encounter

Diane LeBeau

AUTHOR'S CREDENTIALS

A photo of Diane LeBeau.

Diane LeBeau is a metaphysical teacher and counselor in her business, Starlight Enterprises, since 1985.

She lectured at colleges and organizations since 1980.

She appeared on local and national radio and television as a psychic and a singer.

She is a BMI songwriter.

She did psychic readings for many years at psychic fairs put on by nonprofit organizations such as Dewitt Kiwanis Club.

She owned and operated a modeling studio in Hollywood, California, from 1958 to 1964.

She warmed the horses up at Vernon Downs racetrack for the jockeys.

Preface

These are true stories about God, ghosts, Jesus, and a UFO encounter. You may find my stories hilarious, frightening, unbelievable, or amusing, but, hopefully, interesting.

Have you ever: Felt something touch you but no one was around? Had something real heavy move across the room by itself? Heard a voice call your name in the room when no one was around? Seen a physical-looking person in daylight, then disappear right in front of you? Had water splash on you in the home when there was no one around and you were not near water? Seen someone stand by your bed then vanish? Found something in your house with no explanation of where it came from? Thought of a person you haven't seen for years and then they call you? Are you afraid to tell anyone about your unusual or paranormal experiences because you feel they would think you are crazy? Have you ever put something on tape and not hear anything odd while you are making the recording, but when you play it back you hear something sounding like a ghost, like breathing and moaning in back of what you're saying? Have you ever seen an apparition before you knew they passed over? Have you ever had a UFO control your car? These are some of my stories that are in my book.

Definition of Terms

This will explain what some of my words mean as I am using them in this book.

Demonstration:	Answered prayer.
Manifestation:	Make apparent.
Light:	Awareness or visible light.
Angels:	Spirits that communicate within to help us.
Metaphysics:	The dictionary explanation is: A branch of philosophy that deals with the real nature of the universal laws.
He, God:	I use the word He for God, but God is a phenomenal power. It is hard to describe, but it is well worth searching for. Go within.

My Childhood Experiences

The first incident I remember after I was born is my mother carrying me around in a pink blanket when I was about three years old. And I was thinking, "Where am I? Where did I come from? And what am I doing here?"

My parents owned a grocery store, boat harbor, and had gas pumps so they didn't have much time to spend with me. And while I was alone so much I began listening to what I considered wisdom from a very intelligent spirit, because it would inform me of the people coming into the grocery store about when they were going to die. After a few predictions were correct, my mother would say, "How on earth did you know?" And I would say, "I don't know, a spirit told me." I remember now, when I was about nine years old I told my mother the house next door would burn down, and a few days later it happened. Just for the record, no, I had no part in it.

I feel at that young age I had angels watching over me. I was out in the harbor swimming with poison black water snakes, great big snapping turtles, and dog fish. They never harmed me, but one day my sister, Eleanor, and I went out in a rowboat and one of the dog fish jumped into the boat. My sister got the boat to the shore really quick. I jumped out and the dog fish chased me through the parking lot. He had legs and big teeth, and, thank God, I ran faster and I lost him, because they bite people.

When I was fifteen I had a premonition my father would not be able to take me babysitting on Saturday morning. He went to bed Friday night and passed away about three o'clock on Saturday morning. He was sixty three years old, and was riding a water bike the day before, no signs of illness.

My parents were not religious, nor did they show any signs of ESP, although I found out later that my mother and grandmother were tea leaf readers. Also, I found out that my sister, Arlene, was born with a veil over her face, which was supposed to mean she was psychic. I found out later in life she predicted many things for me that were very unusual and true. And in that era there were no radio or television talk shows. In retrospect I feel my intuition and messages I received were definitely by a higher intelligence.

When I was sixteen years old a man named Joe came to the harbor to go boating, and I got to know him. He asked me to marry him, and so I did. The apartment my husband and I rented in Syracuse, New York was haunted, because it was right next door to a nursing home, and I could look out my window and see them carrying out bodies. After we went to bed at night we would see orbs that looked like Casper the ghost. They would swoop down on us and we would cover our heads with the blanket. Also, a door in the attic would open by itself and squeak, and I would hear a man moaning. I found out from the landlord that a man had hung himself in that room. So when my in-laws asked us to go to Los Angeles, California I jumped for joy.

My Encounter with a Serial Killer

After moving to California, due to the fact my husband could not find work at first, I got a job as a model and opened my own studio on Sunset Boulevard in Hollywood, California for amateur and professional photographers. I did all the work myself so I was pretty busy. For a while everything was going well. Then one day a model came into my studio for work. I told her I didn't need anyone for studio work, but since I didn't want to go out on location, I hired her for that.

When I went to sleep that night I woke up to a vision of Jesus standing in my hallway with His arms outstretched. At the time I had no idea why I was seeing Him. A couple of days later a man came to my studio to hire a model to go on location. I said, "I do not go out on location, but I just hired a girl who will." He said his name was Frank Johnson. After he paid me and left I called Loraine and said, "I feel there's something about him I don't feel right about, so make sure you tell him you want to leave his license plate number with your landlady to be sure you're safe." But she did not take my advice and just got in his car because she was anxious to work and did not bother to do it. And this is what happened.

He got on the Santa Anna freeway and she asked him where he was taking her. He didn't answer her, but he pulled the car over and pulled a gun on her. She started struggling with him trying to get the gun away from him, and the gun went off and she was shot in the leg. During the struggle the car door opened and they fell out onto the ground. At that time a highway patrol officer was in the area and heard the gunshot. So he went to investigate. He found them struggling on the ground. She told the officer that he pulled a gun on her and tried to kill her, so the officer arrested him. We were the only two models that survived. The story was reenacted on Dragnet, and was published in the LA Times, and a few Detective magazines.

A few days later I got a call from the Person to Person television show. They said they wanted to interview me, saying he had killed over one hundred women. What I did not tell the news people taking the story was about two days before that happened I saw a man that looked like a vision of Jesus. I realized seeing Jesus must have been a warning. I found out that Frank Johnson was really Harvey Glatman, a notorious serial killer. The news people asked me if I thought he should be executed, and I told them no, because I thought he had to be insane to do what he did. When he went to trial, the jury found him guilty, and he was executed in the gas chamber. There is a story written about Harvey Glatman by Michael Newton in a book entitled "Rope." In the book "Rope" they didn't know that I was the real girl that got away because I had a different name, but it was me.

Soon after that I divorced my husband and hired an agent to do theater work. I joined AGVA, the American Guild of Variety Artists. I felt safer burlesque dancing at clubs and doing slapstick comedy in theaters, and I ended up staying in that business for about five years.

Book Title Came in a Dream

Life went by and at the age of twenty six I decided to move back to New York. I lived alone for a while, then, one evening, while I was sound asleep, I had a dream that I saw a book lying on a table entitled "Reach for the Highest Star." I was looking at it thinking, "That sounds interesting." And my sister, Arlene, was in the dream, and she said, "That's your book." When I woke up some spirit said to me, "You will have some unusual experiences to write about."

In the 1980's I was invited to be a guest in the Nationally syndicated show "Woman to Woman". The topic was about models. So I flew by myself to Los Angeles, California, where the show was being taped. During the show I forgot to tell them about my experience with Harvey Glatman just over twenty years earlier.

Through the years I kept having experiences with the power of God. I began writing about them because I knew the experiences would help people to believe in a power that was available to help them with all the challenges in their lives. I guess now I know why I was not killed.

My Miracle Home

Here is a true story that I consider a miracle. I was living in a townhouse with my new husband, which we rented for about six years. I had an Old English sheepdog named Sir Lloyd Lancelot, and was paying extra to keep him. He was my child that I loved, not a dog to me. He never did anything wrong, but some of the neighbors were afraid of his size, and the landlord told us we had to move. And this is what happened.

I called a man I knew as a church member, his name is Dale. He is psychic like I am. He told me I would meet a man who would offer us a place to stay until we could find a place that would take Lloyd. I had a band job coming up, and when I got to the job a stranger came right up to me and said, "Do you need a place to stay?" I looked at him dumbfounded and said, "Yes, I do." And he replied, "My name is Bob, and my wife and I would love to have you."

I put his phone number away and just waited, trying to persuade the landlord to let us stay where we were, but he wouldn't, so I called Dale back and he said, "Go ahead and call the man back who told you he had a place for you to stay." So I did, and we went there, leaving Lloyd with my sister.

A few days later Bob said, "Go get your dawg." He said the word dog in a strange way as a joke. It took us a long time to learn how to pronounce it like he did. We all laughed about it. He and his wife were wonderful people. We stayed there until we found a house that was God sent, and we are still there. To me that was a miracle, because none of the other people that we knew, friends or family, had a place for us.

The other miracle was that there was no way that Bob and Dale could have known each other. I know now that was God's way of making a miracle for me, because I wouldn't have my home that I have now if I didn't have to move. So if you have what you think are negative things happening to you, maybe it will be for your highest good in the end.

Some Ghost Stories and Premonitions

My sister, Arlene, and I were upstairs in her house. We were on twin beds; I was across the room from her when she called my name and said, "Something is fanning me!" So I looked over and this huge, black object that looked like a bird or a big bat was over her waving its wings. I screamed, and her husband came running to the door, and it just disappeared. We never forgot it.

Here is proof of the afterlife for people. I had a friend for many years named Fred. He wore Timberline boots, and his jeans rolled up. He knew I was afraid of seeing ghosts, but he passed away in his forties. By then I was married, so not alone. One night I heard a noise and woke up to see a leg with the jeans rolled up, and a Timberline boot. It was his way of telling me he was somewhere still alive.

Here's another story. A man who was the maintenance man of the apartment I had previously rented, I hadn't seen him for a while, so I asked him if he was alive or had passed over. His name was George. A few nights later he appeared at the foot of my bed with his arms crossed. He was looking at me and smiling, and just disappeared. At that time it didn't scare me. I don't know why.

One day, I was lying on the couch at three o'clock in the afternoon when something woke me up and I saw a lady sitting in a chair at my table, in physical form, staring at me. When I went "Ahh," she disappeared, and a voice said to me, "That's Shirley's sister." Shirley was a friend of mine who I tried to help spiritually. I had not seen her for a long time, but my sister kept in touch with her. So I called Arlene and asked her to get a picture of Shirley's sister and send it to me, and it WAS her.

I will never forget this experience because her face is engraved in my mind. I feel this is yet another proof I have of life after life.

Another proof of life-after-life story that I wrote was published by Fate Magazine in their May 1989 issue number 470, called "Pushy Ghost." I believe this story is proof of the afterlife, which will also comfort people who have lost a loved one.

After I got messages over and over again in my mind through the years, I had to pay attention to them when they became a reality. One morning I got up and started to make coffee when a song entitled "I Want to be a Cowboy's Sweetheart" kept playing in my mind. I said to myself, "I sang that song when I was thirteen," and tried to laugh it off. But it kept up until it got my attention, when out of the blue a child's voice said to me, "My nine-year-old brother killed me." It gave me chills.

It got even more scary when in the afternoon I happened to turn on the television, and a child came dancing out on the stage singing "I Want to be a Cowboy's Sweetheart." I kept watching and a photograph of the family was shown, and there was a picture of a child, and someone said, "This is her nine-year-old brother," and I said, "Oh, my God!" This ended up being a nationally publicized case, but I kept it to myself.

Also, one morning shortly after that, a child's handprint was on my window in the wintertime. The child's hand was probably the same girl that told me her brother killed her, because nothing was done about it. When people came to my house they could not even believe what they were seeing.

I had a dream that Natalie Wood was going to drown in two weeks. I told a few people about the dream, and they remember me telling them. Two weeks later the news media came out with the story that she had drowned. She had fallen out of the boat they were on. She was one of my favorite actresses, so I felt very sad about this.

I had a seventeen-year-old daughter, Diana, who grew up with her grandparents on her father's side of the family. They got custody of her because I was a dancer, and in those days the people didn't approve of burlesque dancers. They called me one day and told me to come and get her, so I did. I thought it strange when she kept saying, "I'm not going to die, am I Mom?" And I kept saying no, but I would wonder why she would say that.

One night I had a dream that she was in a car accident, but I did not want to scare her, so I did not tell her. One afternoon Diana, my boyfriend and I were playing cards, and ectoplasm surrounded her. It looked like smoke, but none of us were smoking. We were all looking at her, but saying nothing, we didn't want to scare her.

One night, as she was walking up the stairs to our apartment, a bat flew in her hair, and I knew that was a bad sign. Soon after that Diana and I were watching television around three o'clock in the afternoon on March 14th, 1974, when she looked at me with alarm and said, "Mom, I just saw Aunt Vivian looking at me with a very distraught look on her face." Vivian had died on March 14th, 1973.

Diana described the clothes Vivian was wearing. Diana was not old enough to know about the stockings with the seams in the back of the legs. Those stockings were worn in the 1940's. She also described Vivian's dress, which she had never seen her wear. So I asked my other sisters and they told me yes, she did have a dress like that.

I didn't think too much of the incident because I had seen apparitions since I was around nine years old. But this is what happened:

Diana was working at Vernon Downs race track as a groom for the horses. One of the other grooms asked her to go out to eat. They got into a very bad car accident, and Diana's brain was badly damaged. That happened on May 30th, 1974. Vivian came to warn Diana two months before the accident.

I have witnessed the strength and power of energy. One morning I woke up and could not open my mouth for about a minute. Something was holding it shut. You never forget these strange things.

I laid down on the couch one night and something woke me up, so I looked up, and over the drapes there was a young-looking hand up to the wrist, in mid-air. I stared at it and could not believe what I was seeing, but about two weeks later I fell on black ice in a parking lot and broke my arm in two places. An ambulance had to take me to the hospital. I got a pretty good lawsuit settlement from it. So I guess that's what Spirit wanted me to know.

Years later this happened: I had a heavy television set on a stand that my husband and I could not move ourselves. One day in broad daylight my husband called downstairs to me to come up and see what happened. The stand had moved across the room by itself. We were dumbfounded.

Here is another ghost story. One night while coming home by myself at about eleven o'clock, it was raining hard when a black all-terrain vehicle pulled in front of my car from out of nowhere, it seemed. I had to stop my car. A young man wearing all black clothes with black boots just sat on the machine in front of my car, and just stared at me. I stared back at him in amazement, when he just disappeared in front of my eyes. I got out of my car and looked around, but saw nothing.

I found out later my seventeen-year-old great nephew, named Matthew, was in a car with his brother and two other friends, when they hit a tree going a hundred miles an hour because the gas pedal stuck, and Matthew was killed. He was supposed to go to court on Monday, and he told his mother he could not go because he was going away. He told her three days before the accident. He must have had a premonition. This is why I believe everything must be planned by a higher power, and that is why my sister and I can predict these things.

I never understood why I saw what I did. Why didn't the warning go to someone closer to him in the family?

In the 1970's I was coming home one night at about eleven o'clock. I was driving my car at about fifty five miles per hour, when all of a sudden it began slowing down, and my four-way flashers came on, both of them at once. The flasher unit was inside the glove box, so there was no way I could have touched them by mistake. My friend, named Dan, was sitting in the front seat, and my eleven year old daughter was in the back seat. We looked up and saw a large UFO above us, with lights shining on my car. My car stopped dead, and I couldn't start it. We just sat there a few minutes, staring at it in amazement, and then something shot out of it and took off in one direction. And the other thing, which looked like a saucer, shot straight up and disappeared. Then my car started and I was able to drive home.

When I pulled into my apartment complex, about fifteen miles from the ordeal, the neighbors were all outside excited, they had seen it too. I told them what happened to us.

The news media came the next day and told us there were several reports from other people who had seen it. But they televised our story.

Here is another true incident. One night I was lying on my couch and a voice told me my nephew, Eddie, would be killed in an accident within a year. About a year later, one morning, he told his mother he did not want to go to work, but she did not discourage him, so he went, and was killed on his job site that day. I never understood why the message came to me instead of someone closer to him.

There is no distance in spirit. This is an experience I had which the spiritual books call Clairvoyance, which is a term used for seeing things far away.

In the middle of the night I saw a vision of my mother lying on the floor. She was wearing a blue dress. I was in New York, she was in California. Later on I found out she had a mild stroke, and the neighbor found her lying on the floor. When she recovered I asked her if she was wearing a blue dress, and she replied, "Why, yes! How did you know?" And I said, "Because I had a vision of it."

I gave this some thought about being far away; it really doesn't matter if someone is sitting next to you, or miles away. We are one with God, and our souls are all connected.

There is no space in spirit, so it doesn't matter how far away our physical bodies are from each other. And it also doesn't matter if the physical body is deceased if we want to communicate. God is the Source of wisdom. Life itself never passes away, it just changes energy.

While I was writing this book my brother, Roy, passed away. This is more proof of the knowledge within our true self. I will repeat the story here. I use to see visions, such as a fresh grave or things like that, and didn't know why.

I had not seen or heard from my brother in a few months, when I dreamt I saw a body lying on a stretcher with a tag on the toe, and right after that I saw a door with a glass window, and on the other side was a bright light. Somehow Spirit said Roy will pass through this door. When I awoke I told my husband, "I had a dream and it wasn't a good omen. I think Roy is going to pass on to the other world." Within a few days my sister, Eleanor, called me and told me he had passed away.

I had a client named Melanie. She came in for a card reading one day and I told her that I saw her in a bad accident, and it looked like she was going to die, but she would be brought back to life. Soon after that, it did happen. She came in again, and told me about it. She even brought me a picture of the car all smashed up. The spirits told her it wasn't her time yet, and she had to go back. But, even though she was getting married soon after, she didn't want to come back because she was so peaceful there.

It is not the first time I had heard this story from people who had been brought back. This is just the kind of information that helps people who are grieving, because they want to know that their loved ones are at peace.

This is how I began paying attention to my inner spirit guides. When my hand would itch I always got money from somewhere. One day It told me to go buy a scratch-off ticket, and I said, "How am I supposed to know when to go?" And It said, "You will." So I waited until I was told to go to Wegmans. I put my money in the machine, and out came a ticket, and it was worth about ten times the money I paid for it. This is what makes me have a love for God. It also makes me wonder why it doesn't happen to everyone.

This is another incident that really happened to me, and I am not proud of myself, but I want to tell you of my mistake so you won't feel so bad when you do something stupid like me. Ha ha!

It was the Friday before Easter Sunday and I was looking at the race horses on my computer, and I saw a trifecta with the horses' names Easter Gift and Small Token. So I said, "**That's it!** They want to reward us bettors." This will run on Saturday because on Easter there are no races, OTB is closed. So on Saturday I went over there to play it. And guess what? I didn't because there were a lot of horses in the trifecta, so I flat bet Easter Gift by itself. The next day when I looked at the results and it paid $34,750 I was devastated. Because, you see, when I play trifectas I always wheel them down. Wheeling them down means I would put Easter Gift, Small Token, all, then put Easter Gift, all, Small Token. I would have had it, because it came in the second way. I had to either trust God or let fear have its way. I guess I learned a big lesson. I let fear have its way. So I'll never do that again. But many times the Spirit of God tells me what horses to play ahead of time. I have listened to it. People do not understand why it doesn't tell me all the time, and I, myself, cannot explain it.

This is a story about a man that I met that helped me in life when I needed it the most. This is how it happened. I went to the horse races with a man named Joe. He let me drive his car, and he said, "Do not turn it off all the way because I don't have the key." But I forgot and turned it off. So there we were without a ride home. We went into the off track betting parlor and there was a man standing there smiling at me, all dressed up and looking pretty classy, so I said hello to him, quite normal as the bettors do, and he began talking to me. And I told him about our ordeal about not having a ride home and he asked, "Where do you live?" Come to find out, it was on the way to his house, so seeing the other man was with me I felt safe enough to accept the ride.

He said his name was Steve, and we began a friendship. He said he was sixty two years old. He helped me with a lot of things I needed at the time, including helping me start a garden for vegetables.

He got to be about ninety years old and passed away. One day a person named Sharon and I were sitting in my car waiting for the door to open to go in and make some bets. We were watching the cars coming in to park, and one of the cars had three men in it. Well, two of the men got out, and the third man looked familiar. He was smiling at both of us, and Sharon said, "That looks like Steve." He looked like Steve at the age of sixty two when I had met him years ago. I was so surprised, when he just vanished. We asked the other two men about the incident, and they said, "There was no other man in the car with us!"

The Toy Mouse That Duplicated Itself

This true story is something that I cannot explain. On March 30, 2016, when I got up around 5am in the morning, I saw my cat, Tippy, playing with a toy mouse. He was very excited. He was throwing it up in the air. I knew, without a doubt, I had never seen it before, so I asked the other person in the house, and he said no. He was quite amazed, like I was. I thought maybe he bought it for him without telling me.

Well, anyway, we got in the car to go pick up someone, which only took fifteen to twenty minutes, and when we got back home the girl said, "Where did Tippy get the two new toys?" And I said, "WHAT!", and looked, and there were two identical mice. I am telling you, Tippy only had one when we left the house.

We had little plastic balls in the house, and we were always taking a flashlight to look for them under the television set, and so on. So we know, without a doubt, these toys had no way of being here. We also know that no one would have left him a toy without telling us.

Proof of the After Life for Animals and Some Predictions

Arnold the pig sitting in the grass.

Arnold the pig lying on the couch with a blanket.

My sister told me I would own a pig someday. When I was young I used to watch "Green Acres" on television, but my sister did not know that. Well, I fell in love with the pig, whose name was Arnold, and I said to God, "When that pig passes on I want him if he is reborn." Years later my husband and I were going for a walk when something said to me out of the blue, "Time to get your pig." So I repeated it to my husband,

"I want a pig." And he said, "Are you crazy?" And I repeated, "I want a pig."

Well, one day soon after that I was watching the news and saw a man who owned some animals in the city who needed to get rid of them. So I called him and said, "Do you have a pig?" And he said, "No, but I know a lady who has one to sell, and she will even deliver him to you."

So the lady brought him to us, and he weighed seventeen pounds, and was so cute, he ran over to my husband, cuddled up to him as if to say, "Don't let them take me back!" Well, we fell in love with him head over heels, and paid the woman for him and took possession. We took him to department stores and we bought him a leather coat and biker hat. Everywhere we took him people had a million questions, but we were so proud of him, we loved the attention.

We called the local news and they were interested, and did quite a few stories about him, the first being that he was a Babe look-alike. Mike Price, a local television personality, did the story. Our pig would follow the cameraman around and I thought, "Wow! Maybe he IS the Arnold that was on Green Acres." But that is something we will never know. But we did name him Arnold. When he got old enough we had him neutered. He was quite easy to train, we never had trouble.

Pigs are very clean animals and make wonderful pets, and I despise the judges on television who make remarks about dirty people being pigs.

As the years went by he knew how much we loved him. We kept him inside the house unless we took him out. He would love to have his belly rubbed, so we would put our back massager on his stomach. We wish now that we would have put it on Facebook. He would even say "Mama" if we tried to get him to do something he didn't want to do.

Well, when he got sixteen years old he became ill and we could not save him, and he passed away. Soon after his death he began leaving one of his pig hairs where I was sitting, or even in my brand new car. In fact, one day I was going into Off-Track Betting to play my horses, when he left his hair on the armrest of my car door. The name of one of the horses was something about a pig. I was excited so I played it, and it paid pretty good money. This is something I will never forget, because from then on every time something good was going to happen he would leave his pig hair where I could find it.

Are you thinking what other people thought, that the hairs must have been in my house yet? No, that is impossible. At that time we had no other animals in the house either, so we know he somehow was leaving them to let us know he is alive somewhere and it is a comfort to us. It's almost five years later and he is still leaving them. Like I said before, I have a business called Starlight Enterprises, and some of my clients fell in love with him while he was alive. I have a picture of him downstairs in my office, and some of my clients will say to the picture, "Arnold, leave me a hair." When they get up to leave, the hair will be under their chair, and they knew it wasn't there when they sat down.

I believe that our lives are programmed by a higher power, otherwise how could my sister, Arlene, and I predict some of these things that happened. Here are some of the things that she predicted. We used to write songs together, and we wrote a song called "I'm Afraid to Try," which was recorded by Charlie Wiggs in Nashville, Tennessee, and the song got in Billboard magazine. It was played on WSEN radio station in Baldwinsville, New York. The disc jockey that played it told us he was having a party at Maple Grove, and invited us to go. And my sister said to me, "You are going to meet a man there, his name is Chuck, and he has a dog named Goldie, and you will be married before Christmas." This was in November, so I thought, how could that be?

When I got to Maple Grove, I was just sitting alone at a table by myself, and I wanted to dance. So I asked the waiter to go ask the man with the dark hair if he would come and dance with me. So he came over to ask me to dance, so I said to him, "What is your name?" And he said, "Chuck." And I said, "Do you have a dog named Goldie?" And he said, "How do you know? Do you know me?" And I said, "No, I don't." I didn't want to tell him what my sister said because I thought it would scare him. But he did ask me for my phone number. I gave it to him and he did call me, and we did get married before Christmas. However, it only lasted two years, and we got a divorce.

A few years later my sister told me that I would meet a man who says "chooch." Well, I did meet a man who says "chooch." Here is what happened.

One night my sister, Arlene, and I went to a place called Anthony's Manor to see a singer who was playing and singing there. We wanted to get another song recorded for Nashville. A man who played the steel guitar walked through the door and a spirit said to me, "That's your next husband." As it turned out, I asked the man, named Reggie, if he would record some demos for me. It took him quite a while because my sister and I had quite a few songs, so we got to know each other and decided to get married. And he was the man who said "chooch." And that is why I believe that there is a higher power controlling parts of our lives.

I also found out there is really nothing lost in spirit because I have found a few things that I thought were lost by asking Saint Anthony where they are, and he would show me. So one day I saw my neighbor outside with a couple of friends, and they were talking loudly about her ring being lost somewhere in the grass, and I thought maybe I should go out and see if I could help her. Well, I guess it was the Higher Power talking to me, because as soon as I got outside I went right over to it in the grass and said, "Oh, here it is!" And they could not believe it. But I knew then that it's something higher than me that is using me for a channel. And I said to God, "Thank You."

In the middle of the night I get messages and here are some of them that I will explain to you.

A person doesn't have to be psychic to learn to read cards. My sister taught me when I was a teenager. I read a regular deck that is used to play poker and other games. I have a client pick out fifteen cards from the deck and I lay them out in a special way. It makes a difference how they lay as to the meaning of them. It is still a mystery to me why our life can be told from a deck of cards, but I have tested them for forty years, and all I can say is the accuracy is uncanny. Some of the things I have predicted are: if a person is going to court, talk to a policeman, get extra money, a better job, have a death in the family, or have an accident, go to a hospital, get a divorce, ... it's all in the cards. There are **good** things too.

For psychometry, I use a picture of a person and look at the eyes, because the eyes are the window of the soul. Then you need to be psychic. From the picture I can tell about the character of the person. This is sometimes called channeling. Sometimes I cannot know if I am right with what I am getting, because it comes in so fast. But from experiences it has been accurate. I feel the Universal Mind knows all, I never take the credit. I am a vessel. I also believe the people that come to me are supposed to for a higher purpose. I always pray that they are helped because of their visits with me.

In the crystal ball I see images. For instance, I saw a picture of a dog when one of my clients was getting a reading. I told her she was going to get a dog, and she said no. But before she came back she was already given the dog, and she was very excited. I told her the dog would have a black head and face, and he did, and the rest of his body was white.

I told another client the same thing. She would get a dog, because I saw a dog in the crystal ball again. She also said no, but she got the dog the same night, because her boyfriend brought it to her.

I can also see a corpse in the crystal ball when there is going to be a death, and the client always tells me I'm right. If a person comes to me and tells me not to tell them certain things, then I don't. I keep them to myself.

Arnold and Health Mantras

Here are some mantras to help condition your mind. In the middle of the night, soon after adopting Arnold, Spirit gave me a mantra using his name. So, here is a mantra using Arnold:

Awareness of the angels

Remember to rely on spirit

No to negative thinking

One source only

Let go of your problem

Dwell on God's presence

Awareness of the angels: Communication, listen to the inner messages as they come to you. Somehow you will know what is right. It just feels right.

Remember to rely on spirit: This means not to rely on the channels, always stay focused on where the channel comes from.

No to negative thinking: Because the negative energy works against you, and the only power it has is the attention you yourself give it. So don't give it attention.

One source only: There is one source, the Creator. Your connecting to your higher consciousness is your one source.

Let go of your problem: Don't think about the problem, keep thinking about the solution. If you feel anxious, think of something entirely different for a while.

Dwell on God's presence: Work within on feelings of faith that good will happen. Keep knocking or searching, and one day, like a thief in the night, it will appear and make itself known to you. And, just as is promised, you will get your rewards.

Here is another mantra that came to me a little later on, using the word "health."

Heavenly thoughts, peace and love

Elevate your consciousness

Assure yourself of only good to come

Let go of the past and focus on now

The truth sets you free

Health is a state of mind

As you practice these mantras, and the other lessons in this book, you will find your abilities grow, and that you are better able to utilize the Infinite Wisdom to gain health, and, yes, inner happiness.

When you start thinking of a problem it may help to go over the Arnold mantra instead. This came to me in the middle of the night, so I wrote it down right away. I showed it to some of my friends and they told me they loved it and told me it did help them. Anything that keeps our mind off worry or negativity, and replaces our thinking with something that makes us feel good is very important.

IMPORTANT

The contents of this book need to be absorbed by your subconscious mind. You need to pay more attention to the Ten Power Tools and the Meditations. It is best to read them over and over just before sleep and first thing in the morning. It takes time to raise your consciousness before you see results in your outer conditions. Pay more attention to your inner self and less attention to your problems. You will be rewarded for your efforts. You already know negative thinking has no benefits. Focus on what you want, not on what you don't want.

Bible References

The Bible has very deep meanings and we need to soul-search in order to fully understand the writers. Here is a list of the Bible passages used in this book.

Psalms 91:1	He that dwells in the secret place of the most high shall abide under the shadow of the Almighty.
Matthew 6:33	Seek ye first His Kingdom and His righteousness, and all these things shall be added unto you.
Hebrews 11:1	Faith is the substance of things hoped for, the evidence of things not seen.
Mark 11:24	Believe you will receive and you will.
Psalms 46:10	Be still and know that I am God.
Matthew 6:19-20	Lay not up for yourselves treasures upon earth, ... but lay up for yourselves treasures in Heaven.
Matthew 7:24	Build your house on a rock, not on sand.

Genesis 1:27	God created man in His Own Image and Likeness.
John 3:3	Except ye be born again you cannot enter into the Kingdom of Heaven.
John 8:32	Ye shall know the truth and the truth shall set you free.

The Ten Power Tools

I never was one to read the Bible at first, but after I studied metaphysics, I found these Bible references to be so important in my life. What is interesting to me is, they were all written by different prophets or apostles. And yet they give the same message. I used them to keep myself in tune so I could write this book.

Prayer should be practiced on a daily basis. Don't wait until an emergency arises, because remember, our demonstration depends on an expansion of our consciousness. An expansion of consciousness means to understand something better, or in other words, realize something with more clarity.

Now, let's go over the Bible passage "Power Tools" one at a time.

"He that dwells in the secret place of the most high shall abide under the shadow of the Almighty." The secret place is withdrawing your attention from your outer world. It promises that you will be given direction from doing this. The secret place is deep within you, your own "I am." Never use your "I am" in a negative way. If you say "I am poor" or "I am sick" long enough, you will believe it, and that is your secret place.

You have heard people say God can do *for* you what He can do *through* you. You want prosperity and health, don't you? Your "I am" is a wonderful power tool when used in a positive way.

"Seek ye first the Kingdom of God and His Righteousness, and all these things shall be added unto you." It means seek the consciousness of God, or good. Seek love, seek peace, within your mind. Let go of your anger toward another who has hurt you. Letting go really helps *you*. It promises you if you let go of your anger and judgments, you will be rewarded.

"Faith is the substance of things hoped for, the evidence of things not seen." *Faith itself* is the answer to your highest good. Faith in Spirit of God, or good. What has helped me is keeping my own opinions on where it will come from out of my mind. *Faith itself* will bring you money because faith is the very substance that you need to receive it.

"Believe you will receive and you will." When you pray and get results, you will have more faith next time.

"Be still and know that I am God." God is stillness, not turmoil. Your "I am" needs to be silenced. When you silence your "I am" you have more intuition. Intuition is from your Higher Self. Extra Sensory Perception. To perceive something extra, higher. I know *my* psychic abilities are interrupted when my mind is emotional. That is why I say to my clients, I need to be "tuned in" so to speak, before I can answer your questions, because my lower self is not able to receive messages when it is influenced by outer conditions. The wisdom is always there waiting for you to accept it.

"Don't lay treasures on earth, ... but lay treasures in Heaven." Put your heart on loving Love, not loving your new home or new car. Love spirit of peace, do not love your pride. Remember, Heaven and hell are states of mind. The treasures in Heaven, or your "I am," can never be stolen by another person like personal possessions can.

"Build your house on a rock, not on sand." Your house is your consciousness. You need to build your faith on your spirit instead of building your faith on outer things, such as a job, which you could lose. If you put your faith in anything material, or what you can see, that is building your house, or your consciousness, on sand. Sand can sink. If you place your faith in one person, that person may let you down. Your real security is believing that your Creator is the one source from which all your good comes.

"God created man in His Image and Likeness." God is the Creator, so if He created you in His Own Image and Likeness, then you are a creator of your outer conditions. But God is Infinite Wisdom Itself, so I learned it is better to trust that wisdom, instead of your plans.

"Except ye be born again you cannot enter into the Kingdom of Heaven." First, your body is born. When you are born again, that is your spirit that is born. Your spirit needs to be made new. God is love. Your spirit needs to be born again in love. In other words, change your thinking. I have known people who take pride in being stubborn, or getting even. But what they do not realize is they are bringing negative conditions in their own lives by thinking those kinds of thoughts.

"Ye shall know the truth, and the truth shall set you free." I asked several of my clients to explain this, and they laughed and said, "I just don't know. I never bothered to think about it." This truth is the very truth that sets you free. Free from worry, freedom from having to make decisions. Freedom from fear. Getting to know your own relationship with your Creator will set you free. The outer conditions in our lives are a mirror reflection of what we believe. We cannot always believe what we want to believe. We may say, "I want to be a millionaire, so I want to believe this so I can create it." It needs a lot of inner work. You start with smaller things that you know you can create. As you see your demonstrations happen, your own faith increases and your prayers get answered sooner.

Knowing what the truth is isn't enough. You have to practice it, not part of the time, but live it all of the time. It is not enough to know that God is love. You need to let it express itself through you. The only power for good needs to be born in your spirit, and you are the only one that can remind yourself to keep your mind on good each day, each moment. To know the truth is what heals to the extent that such truth is realized by the thinker. It is expanding your consciousness. Remember, there is *no* opposing force outside yourself keeping you from your highest good. Don't waste your time chasing after outer things to make you happy.

There is no opposing force against you. You need to detach your mind from others and work on yourself. A positive state of mind needs to be focused on every waking moment, not just prayer time. You need to realize God's power is above all problems, and you need to let go and keep thinking about that power and surrender to it. You need to listen to that All-Knowing wisdom within you and do what feels right.

What I Believe

Due to the fact that there are too many negative influences for all of us to deal with, this book may be a helpful tool to enforce some positive influences to counteract the negative ones.

Sooner or later we all come to the conclusion that some of the material things we search for in life are a disappointment after we obtain them. We find we need God in our lives, and this book will help you to connect on a more personal level with the Creator. This is how happiness and security become more permanent.

I believe that God is energy and the Creator of the universe, and all living things. I believe we are all connected to it and each other through our thoughts and feelings. God is pure Intelligence, Love, and the real Source of everything good that we want in our lives. But we need to stay connected to it by believing in it.

This love energy beats our hearts, grows our finger nails, and so on, in silence. It is inside our minds for us to connect to, and all life forms have it. Here is a true story in regards to this.

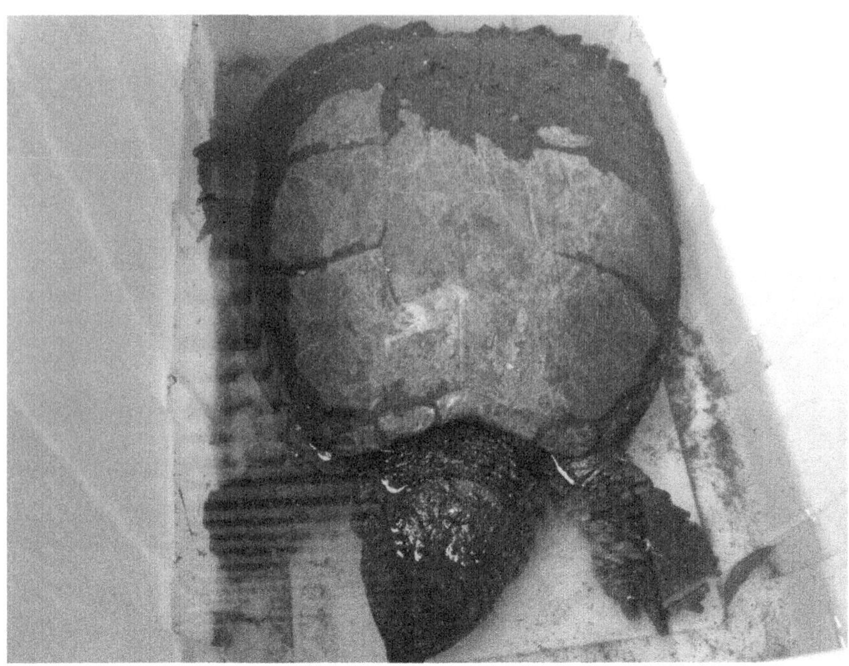

We were on our way home from a friend's house when my husband, Reggie, and I saw a great big snapping turtle trying to get across the road. So I told him to stop the car, because I love turtles and I didn't want the turtle to get run over. But the turtle got in the road anyway, and wouldn't move. So much to my surprise, Reggie picked it up. And, usually, snapping turtles will bite you, but it didn't snap at all. So he put it on the grass and it just sat there. I said, "I'm not going to leave him or her out here, we have to help somehow.

I said a prayer asking God what to do, when a neighbor who was watching us said, "I will bring out something for you to put the turtle in so you can take it with you." The man brought a storage bin out, just the right size for the turtle, and Reggie picked it up and put it in the bin, and still the turtle didn't show any signs of being afraid or angry, which is very unusual, because I have had a lot of experiences with those kinds of turtles. So we brought it home and waited until morning, and again we asked Wisdom for help. And it showed us a safe place to put it in the water where no one can get to it. The only time the turtle opened his or her mouth to him is when it thought Reggie was going to put it back in the storage bin. So we took a picture and put it on Facebook, and we consider this a miracle. That's why I put the picture in this book. We named her G.G. for Good Girl.

We need to feel love, and not dwell on anger, fear, jealousy, or our problems of any kind, because if we do, we are the ones who give these things more power to work against our relationships, our peace of mind, and our prosperity in our personal lives. This different way of thinking takes awareness and practice, but if we begin to feel its presence by replacing our negative thoughts with thoughts of love, kindness, and what we can do for others, our personal problems will disappear. I believe this is our true savior, or our connection to our own higher self. When people try to find pleasure in drugs, alcohol, or gluttony, it disconnects them from their source.

I believe that only our bodies die, but in reality there is no death in spirit. I believe life is a school, and we learn through our experiences, whether negative or positive, and our soul stores our wisdom for eternity.

But I believe we can be taught positive soul growth through these experiences if we allow ourselves to realize the benefits from negativity and what these things have taught us.

Here is what life's experiences have taught me. Even though I had the excitement of modeling in Hollywood, and being an exotic dancer, actress, and singer - living the dream a lot of girls have - marrying the man of my dreams, sexual thrills? WOW! Having all the money I wanted, I still ended up having melancholy, which is a medical term for a sadness you can't get rid of, no matter what you do, or where you go. I knew I had to learn more truth about God, so I read books by James Van Praugh (who had experiences similar to mine), and Deepak Chopra. But the book that helped me the most was "Make Your Life Worthwhile," by Emmit Fox, a book that Dell Powers, a Unity minister, gave me, back when I was twenty three years old. I read it every morning and every night before going to sleep. Was it wrong for me to experiences these things? I know now that these life experiences were needed for me to grow in truth.

If I can master getting rid of melancholy after all I've been through, I believe you can too.

Being At Peace with Yourself

Have you read a lot of the spiritual books on the market and still find that your personal life hasn't changed? I hope I can make a difference, but you need to do a lot of inner work yourself. I'm not going to tell you this is easy. There is an old saying, you can lead a horse to water, but you can't make him drink.

Ok, are you ready to focus on what I'm telling you? Go get comfortable and relax. Intellectual knowledge is great, but you need awareness as to what is going on within your thinking, because you are the Captain of your own ship, and your consciousness is where you start. Sound too simple? Well, you will see it's not as simple as it sounds.

Have you a problem that's bothering you and you realize if you could only forget the problem, you would be at peace? So you struggle to forget. It gets worse, because we are energy beings, and fighting a thing only gives it more power against you.

We create our outer conditions in our little or big world. We create what we believe. The problem is a lot of what's going on is sometimes unconscious or subconscious, because we are not aware. So the first step is awareness. Yes, I repeated myself ... awareness. Our subconscious is actually our connection. We cannot work directly on our subconscious; we need to work on our consciousness by repetition. If you repeat something over and over every day, you begin to get feelings stirred up. What happens is we will receive what the books call an expansion of consciousness, or a realization.

When we get a desire manifested, or put in other words, when we get a prayer answered, it is called a demonstration. It is brought about by faith. Faith is believing. We cannot always believe what we want to, that's why we need to repeat affirmations. You have maybe read somewhere that you need to detach. The reason for that is because anxiety is a negative energy, or put in layman's terms, a negative feeling or state of mind. So keep focused on your affirmation, and let go.

Let's start with a demonstration of prosperity. This is how you do it. Every day say, "I am getting money from somewhere. I don't know where or how it is coming to me, but I believe it will." Actually, the money will come from your spirit, but it will find a channel that is right for you.

But you need to correct your old beliefs about lack, because those thoughts will work against your positive ones. Do you say, "I would buy that, but I can't afford it." You need to get rid of those kinds of ideas. Those thoughts are your only enemies. There is no other opposing force out there working against you. Some people will say to me, "I am on welfare." or "I am on disability." or "I only make so much from my job." That may be true, but you created that. If you want to change that scenario, change your ideas. Your life can not be changed by begging God for thirty minutes a day. You need to change every negative thought that you have, every waking moment, from now on, to see a difference. You cannot focus on your outer picture and worry. You need to go within and work very hard on keeping your mind on your affirmations. And, focus on what you want, not on what you don't want. This does not just apply to money.

Affirmations and Meditations

The following meditations and affirmations are what helped me the most. They are truth principles to affirm daily:

My awareness of God *as* my supply *is* my supply.

Wealth is already mine.

I am healthy.

I am in God's Presence now.

My consciousness of truth is the substance for all that I want.

My consciousness of truth brings wealth now.

The Master within guides me with its wisdom.

My emotion is under the control of the Master.

Spirit is my source of wealth.

I accept my highest good.

My "I am" is creating all good.

There is *no* opposing force.

I let go of yesterday's mistakes.

I am busy doing what I love.

My realizations are becoming clear today.

My living Master is everything to me.

Today I have the power now ... now ... everything is now.

I am creating peace within, all is in order.

My "I am" is the unlimited source.

The Master loves me, and I am healed.

I am guided what to eat by the wisdom within, I desire the food that is good for me.

Infinite wisdom is directing me.

These affirmations heal me ... I am perfect.

Do You Know Your Subconscious Mind?

Your subconscious is what stores up everything you have ever learned in the past. Say you have learned how to roller skate or ride a bicycle. Years later you can pick up right where you left off. Your subconscious can also store up your mistakes and sins. As I said before, you always know when you do something that you feel in your heart is not right. Your subconscious is what brings about your troubles. So it is important to be on guard at the door of your thoughts.

Say you listen to a television commercial: "The cold and flu season is here." You accept that as true, and without even realizing this, you begin to think about the flu. With this thinking, you are giving the flu power, and what manifests in your body? Right! Flu! That is why it is so important to think about the nature of God, which is Love, Life, Power, Peace, Health, Truth, etc., because then those are the things that will manifest for you. Why? Because thoughts are power.

Dominion lies within your own thinking. "We are spiritual beings," "God created us in His Own Image and Likeness" (Genesis 1:27). He gave us power to choose. Our feelings are up to us. But we must remember God is our Partner, and choosing to worship Him, He will protect us from all harm. Power is a force, not just a word. Power gives the earth gravity, electricity gives us light, and the Power of God gives us peace of mind, and all good in our lives. We worship Him in spirit within our own thinking and feelings. So don't look up and away outside for Him. We can see with our eyes only the manifest results of God, such as the sunshine, rain, flowers, stars, trees, birds, animals, and people. But we must worship God, Who created these things, not the things.

When we want a material thing on earth, let us remember, God is the Source of bringing that material thing into reality for us. Never dwell on the material thing and beg God. You don't need to. Seek the Kingdom. God is Intelligence. He knows what you want and need to bring complete happiness and contentment into your world. Just let Him, or It.

Now, let's get back to your subconscious. That will cause you trouble if you have been committing any sins. Why? Because it can make you feel not worthy of receiving your good. "And we know that to them that love God, all things work together for good" (Romans 8:28). God acts on belief and faith. If you cannot believe you can receive, you won't. And if you feel guilty, you won't feel you deserve good.

Where pride and intellect are dominant, there is little room for opportunity for the subconscious to do its' cleansing work. Affirm, "I am no longer in bondage to personality."

We are Spirit, Soul, and Body. The mistake made by many students is the will ignores any power higher than itself.

Therefore, pride is harmful. You cannot put new wine in an old wine bottle. Figure this out:

Your consciousness must be the "I Am" of you, not some power outside your "I Am." Do not say "I am" anything that you do not want in your life, such as "I am sick, tired, depressed, lonely, bored, or angry." It may take time to change your outer life, so start now. Say what you want to make happen, instead of affirming negative ideas.

God is Love. This does not mean emotion, and it does not mean your human ego self must struggle with this. The Love is always available to you, a gift when you were born.

So those are the important parts of my life's story up until now. Even though the variety of careers I had did not make me feel fulfilled, or get rid of that empty feeling, I do believe the lives we live are preplanned by our Creator for lessons we need on our earth life.

Even though I had all those relationships, I believe they, too, were meant to be. In retrospect, I learned a lot about myself and God from the emotional pain. I believe our souls are eternal, and what we learn is never wasted.

There is a solution contained within every so-called problem we think we can have, and to become aware of our own negativity and correct our own thoughts and feelings about the matter, will correct the outer circumstances.

Therefore, if a person prays for money alone and gets it, the money will not be security or bring contentment.

Nothing material can bring happiness or fulfillment to you unless you understand how your own mind works, and the truth about life and what God really is. So keep praying for understanding yourself and God.

The Truth About God

The truth about God needs to be experienced in the consciousness of the student. We need to focus, and not let our minds wander. Keep bringing it back. The focal point needs to be concentrated on what the truth is about, God, and we need to stop paying attention to outer conditions, because outer conditions are happening because of our own error thoughts from the past or present thinking anyway. Negativity is our fault. We need to get ourselves to believe that God consciousness is what we want, and its perfection is within us already, and our part is to keep ourselves attuned to it with our own determination. Faith is easier to have after knowledge is obtained about oneself and God, so pray for understanding, or what is called realizations. Once you obtain the knowledge and faith, It, or God, will take care of your life's desires, and you can become at peace. I did.

Everything in our world is a manifestation of activity within ourselves, and the conditions and circumstances of our life reflect the states of consciousness we are in.

This is a poem that came to me in 1990, which I sent to a free poetry contest, and was awarded "Honorable Mention". So I wanted to share it with my readers.

Children of Mine

Children of Mine, this is what you must do;
Stop arguing over who is wrong or right,
Even you born-again Christians who
Swear you finally saw the light,
There is only one way you will be set free;
And that's by truly loving others
The same way you love me.